W9-BTQ-554

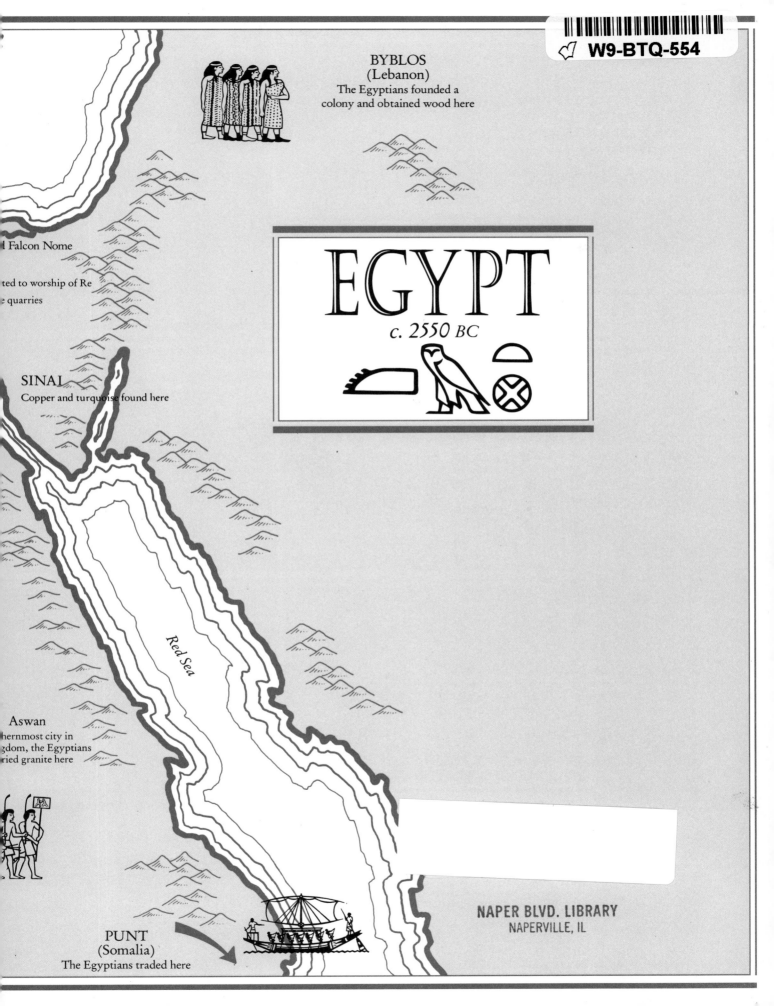

BYBLOS
(Lebanon)
The Egyptians founded a
colony and obtained wood here

d Falcon Nome

ted to worship of Re

e quarries

SINAI
Copper and turquoise found here

EGYPT
c. 2550 BC

Red Sea

Aswan
hernmost city in
gdom, the Egyptians
ried granite here

PUNT
(Somalia)
The Egyptians traded here

NAPER BLVD. LIBRARY
NAPERVILLE, IL

PYRAMIDS
OF ANCIENT EGYPT

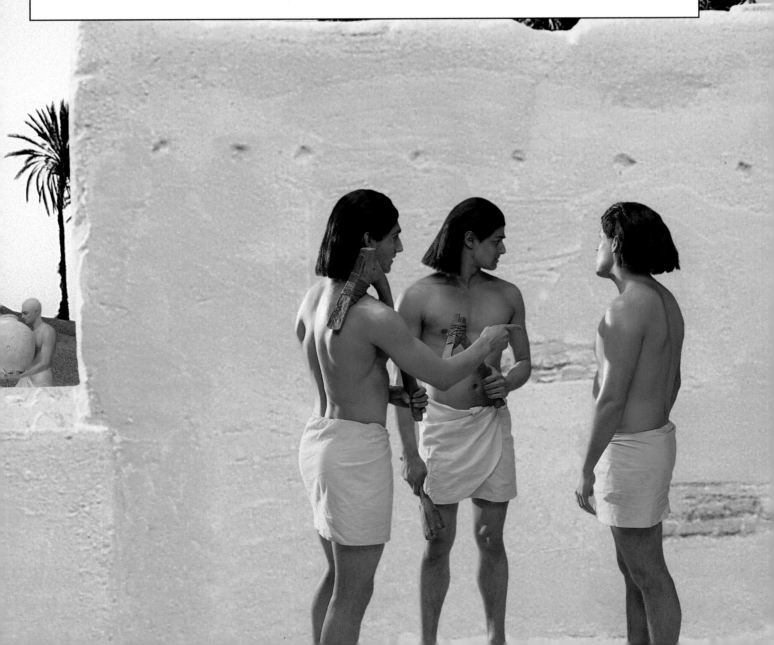

LIVING HISTORY

PYRAMIDS
OF ANCIENT EGYPT

JOHN D. CLARE, Editor

GULLIVER BOOKS
HARCOURT BRACE JOVANOVICH, PUBLISHERS
SAN DIEGO   NEW YORK   LONDON

NAPERVILLE PUBLIC LIBRARIES
Naperville, Illinois

Copyright © 1992, 1991 by Random Century Publishing Group
Limited

First published in Great Britain in 1991 by The Bodley Head
Children's Books, an imprint of The Random Century Group Ltd

First U.S. edition 1992

Created by Roxby Paintbox Co. Ltd

All rights reserved. No part of this publication may be reproduced
or transmitted in any form or by any means, electronic or mechan-
ical, including photocopy, recording, or any information storage
and retrieval system, without permission in writing from the
publisher.

Requests for permission to make copies of any part of the work
should be mailed to:
Permissions Department,
Harcourt Brace Jovanovich, Publishers, 8th Floor,
Orlando, Florida 32887.

Library of Congress Cataloging-in-Publication Data
Clare, John, 1952–
Pyramids of ancient Egypt/John Clare.
p.   cm. — (Living history)
"Gulliver books."
Summary: Describes daily life in ancient Egypt during the time of
the Pharaoh Chephren, including clothing, makeup, home life,
religious practices, burial rituals, and the construction and role
of the pyramids.
ISBN 0-15-200509-9
1. Egypt — Social life and customs — To 332 B.C. — Juvenile
literature.   2. Pyramids — Egypt — Design and construction —
Juvenile literature.   [1. Egypt — Social life and customs —
To 332 B.C.]
I. Title.   II. Series: Living history (San Diego, Calif.)
DT61.C54   1992
932 — dc20   91-11735

Director of Photography   Tymn Lyntell
Photography   Charles Best
Art Director   Dalia Hartman
Production Manager   Fiona Nicholson
Visualization/Systems Operator   Antony Parks
Typesetting   Thompson Type, San Diego, California
Reproduction   F. E. Burman Ltd
                  Columbia Offset Ltd
                  Dalim Computer Graphic Systems U.K. Ltd
                  J. Film Process Ltd
                  Trademasters Ltd

Printed in Hong Kong
A B C D E

ACKNOWLEDGMENTS

Advisors: The British Museum, Department of Egyptian Antiquities;
Dr. Rosalie David. **Costumes:** Joanna Measure, Val Metheringham.
Jewelry: Angie Woodcock. **Makeup:** Alex Cawdron, Caroline Kelly,
Pat Postle, Hilary Steinberg. **Maps:** Simon Ray-Hills. **Models:** Chris
Lovell, Neville Smith. **Props:** Caroline Gardner, Helen Pettit. **Casting
and movement consultant:** Mike Loades assisted by Gordon Summers.
Photographer's assistant: Alex Rhodes. **Picture research:** Valerie
Tongue.

Additional photographs: Reproduced by courtesy of the Trustees of the
British Museum, p. 62 bottom left, p. 63 center left; Antony Parks,
pp. 26–27; Robin Scagell, pp. 30–31; Spectrum Colour Library, pp. 8–9,
42–43, 48–49; Zefa Picture Library, pp. 1–5, 6–7, 40–41.

Contents

Ancient Egypt

Around 4,500 years ago, when people in northern Europe were still living in Stone Age huts and eating berries, a complex civilization flourished in Egypt. The enormous tombs called pyramids that were built for the pharaohs, Egypt's kings, are a

fascinating remnant of that time. Those at Giza were built 1,200 years before the reign of Tutankhamen and 2,500 years before Cleopatra. They were more ancient to Cleopatra than she is to us.

Egypt has been called the gift of the Nile. Ancient Egyptians were drawn to the water and fertile soil of the long, narrow river valley and the broad delta region. The southern part, between Aswan and Giza, was known as *Ta-shema* (Upper Egypt). Here the valley was only 12 miles (20 kilometers) wide at its broadest point, and the weather was hot and dry. On either side of the valley there was a desert called *Deshret* (the Red Land). Five hundred miles (800 kilometers) downriver from Aswan, just north of Giza, the river divided before flowing into the Mediterranean Sea. This delta area, called *Ta-meh* (Lower Egypt), had grassland, marshes, and creeks. Cool breezes and moisture made the climate milder than that of Upper Egypt.

The ancient Greeks were the first people to use the name Egypt. The name is derived from Ptah, a local god of the capital that was founded on the border between Upper and Lower Egypt around 3100 B.C. by King Menes when he united the two.

RELIGION AND BELIEFS

The ancient Egyptians had many gods. Some controlled the natural world; others influenced everyday life. The sun god Re (Ra), who took the sun across the sky in a boat each day, became the most important during the fourth dynasty. Re was the son of Nut, the sky goddess who stretched over the earth, and Geb, the earth god. Re's own children were Shu, the air god, and Tefnut, the goddess of moisture. Among the minor gods were Khnum, the creator of man; Thoth, the inventor of writing; Ptah, the god of craftsmen; Anubis, the undertaker god; and Sebek, the crocodile god.

Osiris, the god of the dead, was worshiped and honored throughout Egypt. The pharaoh's power was associated with Osiris. According to Egyptian legend, Osiris was killed and torn into many pieces by his evil brother, Seth. Isis, Osiris's sister

and wife, collected the pieces and restored him to life long enough for him to father Horus, the protector of Egypt. The Egyptians believed that the pharaoh was the god Horus. While Osiris ruled the dead, the pharaoh, as Horus, ruled the living. Following the example of Osiris, many pharaohs married their own sisters.

Egyptian priests taught that beyond the western horizon lay the Kingdom of Osiris, the subterranean spirit world of the dead. All ordinary Egyptians hoped to dwell with Osiris when they died. Above the skies lay heaven, the land of the gods, ruled over by Re. Only the pharaoh, a god himself, was pure and powerful enough to join the other gods there.

The Egyptians also believed that the spirit remained connected to the body after death. To prepare the dead for the afterlife either in the Kingdom of Osiris or with Re in the sky, they preserved their corpses by mummifying them. Even ordinary Egyptians were mummified, but particular care was taken to preserve the pharaoh's body. In the fourth dynasty the Egyptians prepared for their pharaoh's afterlife by building the pyramids.

THE PHARAOHS

After Menes united Egypt and built the palace of the White Wall, the ruler of Upper and Lower Egypt was called the pharaoh, from the word *per-aa* meaning Great House. The pharaohs who rose to power during the period known as the Old Kingdom (2686–2181 B.C.) were among the most powerful in Egyptian history. Seneferu (Snefru) and his descendants — the pharaohs of the fourth dynasty — built the pyramids at Giza, which were the first true pyramids.

In 2558 B.C. Chephren (Khafre), the grandson of Seneferu, inherited the throne from his father, Cheops (Khufu). Chephren,

the fourth pharaoh of the fourth dynasty, was the head of the government and the chief priest. His commands could not be questioned and his word was law. Chephren was the first ruler to call himself the "great god" and the "son of Re." Like his father, Cheops, who built the Great Pyramid at Giza, Chephren ordered a pyramid to be built during his reign.

Chephren wore two crowns: the red crown of Lower Egypt and the white of Upper Egypt. When he was crowned, Chephren walked around the palace of the White Wall, to the south then to the north. The two crowns showed his lordship over both Upper and Lower Egypt, and by walking around the White Wall, he demonstrated the unity of both.

Every two years Chephren traveled through Egypt on a tour known as the "following of Horus." Sailing along the Nile on the royal barge, he visited each nome, or district, inspecting the accounts of each official. As he traveled, the nobles raised their hands in worship and cried, "Adoration to you, O god. Your people can see how beautiful you are."

7

The Great Pyramid

The first Egyptian pyramid was built by Pharaoh Zoser (Djoser) in the thirtieth century B.C. During the next ten centuries, Egypt's rulers built approximately 90 pyramids. The largest and most famous were built at Giza by Cheops, Chephren, and Chephren's son, Mycerinus (Menkure). Even in the time of the pharaohs, rich Egyptians traveled to Giza to see the Great Pyramid of Cheops.

The Great Pyramid is the largest stone building in the world. It is built from almost two and a half million blocks of lime-stone and granite that weigh between 2 and 70 tons apiece. This is enough stone to build a low wall around the earth. Its 13-acre base is the same size as seven blocks in New York City, and it is as high as a 40-story building. The Great Pyramid is so well constructed that in the nineteenth century when archaeologists explored the inside by blasting tunnels with gunpowder, the 4,000-year-old pyramid did not collapse.

Each pyramid was part of a larger complex, including two temples and in some complexes smaller pyramids, possibly for the queens. Near the Great Pyramid were the smaller *mastabas* (traditional brick tombs) of important nobility.

Building a pyramid required the labor of thousands of people over a period of 20 or 30 years and drained much of Egypt's wealth. But for the ancient Egyptians, a pyramid was far more than a tomb. It was a religious monument. The sloping sides represented the rays of the sun god. Egyptians believed that the dead pharaoh could climb these rays to heaven.

Pharaoh Chephren's pyramid is still under construction, but the Great Pyramid, known to the Egyptians as "the Horizon of Cheops," is finished, and the body of Pharaoh Cheops is buried there. The pyramid stands 481 feet (146 meters) high. Each side measures 756 feet (230 meters). The entrance to the burial chamber, high above ground on the north side, is hidden by casing stones. The pyramid has been built with great precision. The difference between the longest and the shortest sides is less than 8 inches (20 centimeters). The corners are almost perfect right angles (0.09 percent error), and the base is almost perfectly flat (0.004 percent error). The casing stones on the outside of the pyramid are so accurately positioned that it is impossible to push even a hair into the joints.

Egyptian Seasons

All of Egypt depended on the Nile for water, food, and transportation. Because very little rain fell in either Upper or Lower Egypt and when it did rain the water poured down in destructive torrents, the Egyptians took water for farming and drinking from the Nile.

The Egyptian year was divided into three seasons based on the ebb and flow of the river. From June to September was the time of the flood, called *akhet*. After that came *peret*, when the river receded, and finally

shemu, the time of drought.

Beginning with the unification of Egypt, priests using instruments called nilometers measured the flood and recorded their measurements. These records were used to calculate the amount of harvest tax the people would pay. In a good year the Nile rose 27 feet (8 meters) at the palace of the White Wall.

During *akhet,* the Nile washed rich soil across the land. The Egyptians channeled the flood waters onto the fields and dammed them to deposit the mud. The need to maintain dikes and irrigation channels as well as the convenient transportation that the river provided were some of the reasons that Egypt was the first country in the world to have a national government. Egyptians used astronomy to predict the seasons and developed mathematics to measure the flood and rebuild field boundaries.

The peasants built their villages on mounds constructed above the flood. For most of them *akhet* was a time of rest.

It is the time of akhet, *the flood. Melting snow has washed down from the mountains of Cush (Ethiopia) into Egypt, bringing black mud, which fertilizes the soil for next year's harvest. The Egyptians believe that the Nile is a god, and that Khnum, the creator-god, causes the river to swell.*

Farming

From October to February was *peret* (coming forth), the time of planting. The Keeper of the Storeroom distributed seeds that farmers sowed by hand, then covered by plowing the soil. Egyptian farmers grew emmer (a type of wheat), barley, fruit, and vegetables. They also grew flax for linen and papyrus reeds for paper. Because they had no sugar, they collected honey.

During the time of the Old Kingdom, Egyptians kept gazelles, cranes, cattle, sheep, goats, and pigs. They did not domesticate horses or camels until much later.

From February to June was *shemu* (drought), the time of harvest. Laborers worked in "hands" of five men under a *kherp* (the holder of the rod of discipline). Back in the village, oxen trod out grain on a threshing floor. Dirt and dung mingled

with grain and straw. The grain was used to make both beer and bread.

The peasants reap to the music of a flute. They pray to Isis as they work, because the cutting of the barley reminds her of how her husband was cut into pieces. They cut the barley just below the ear (above) and let it fall to the ground, where it is gathered and loaded onto donkeys.

13

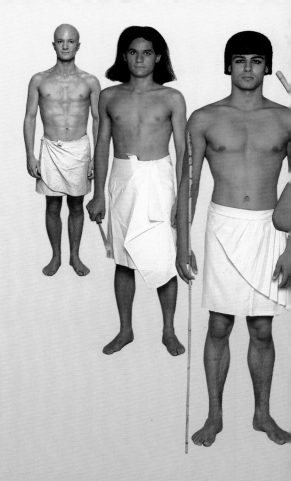

Egyptian Society

Chephren's highest officials, called *imakhu* (friends of the pharaoh), were usually members of the royal family. They led trade missions, commanded the army, and acted as nomarchs (rulers of the nomes). The chief minister, or *tjaty*, was in charge of the Treasury and the House of the Granary (the Department of Agriculture) as well as being the chief judge. Sometimes the pharaoh allowed a favored *imakhu* to build a tomb by the pyramids, where he would receive food offerings for the afterlife.

All government officials were scribes (educated men). Below the *imakhu* were the secretaries, the sandal bearers, the supervisors of the royal meals, and the overseers on the pyramids. Many other scribes were priests in the hundreds of temples to the gods or in the mortuary temples.

On a lower rung of society, the *hemutiu* — craftsmen such as weavers, sculptors, barbers, and laundrymen — provided for the needs of the wealthy. Lower still were the *mertu* (peasants), the majority of the population who were assigned laboring jobs by the House of the Granary. During the Old Kingdom there were no slaves in Egypt, but the *mertu* (on whose labor the whole society depended) had no personal freedom. They had few possessions and could be beaten by those they worked for. When the pharaoh gave land to a noble, the gift included the *mertu* who lived there.

Chephren, wearing a ceremonial gala skirt and a false beard, carries a crook and flail, the tools of a cowherd carried by the god Osiris. These symbolize the pharaoh's duty to rule and tend Egypt. Behind him (right to left) stand his son Mycerinus, a member of the royal family, a scribe (with his stick of authority), an overseer, a craftsman (hemutiu), and a peasant (mertu).

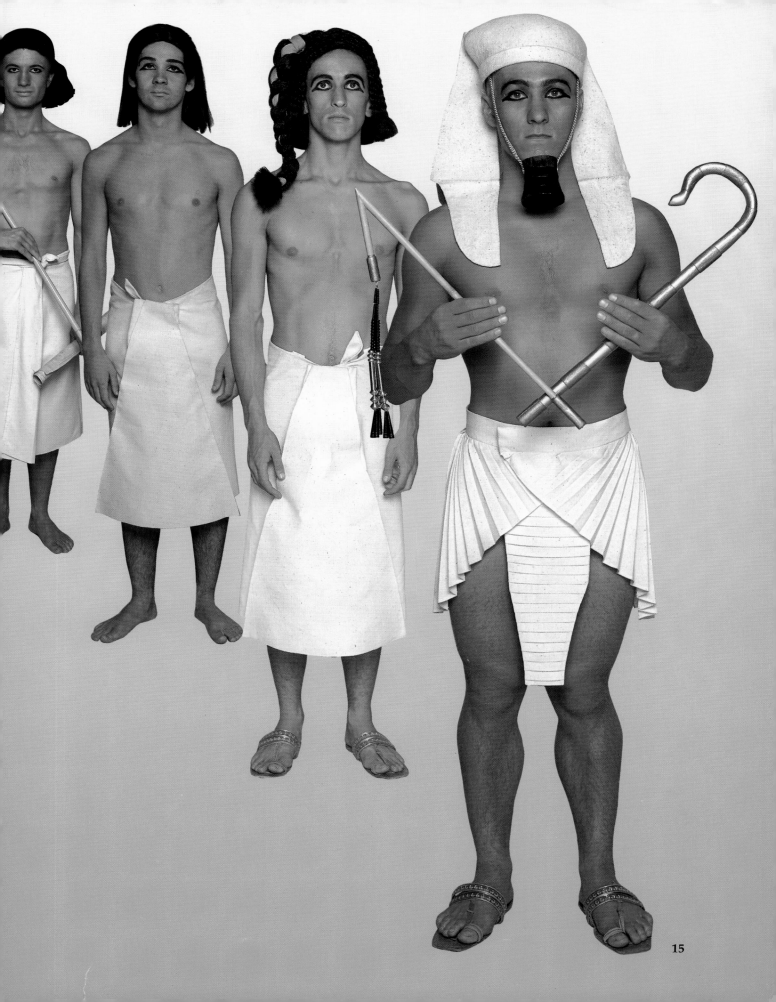

15

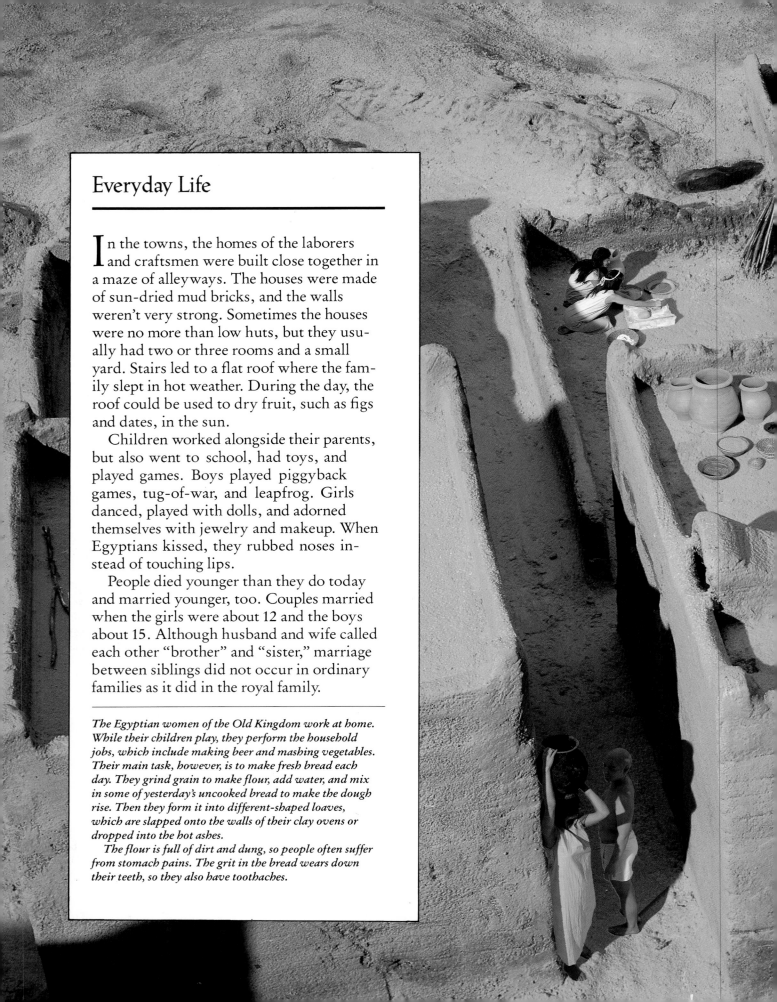

Everyday Life

In the towns, the homes of the laborers and craftsmen were built close together in a maze of alleyways. The houses were made of sun-dried mud bricks, and the walls weren't very strong. Sometimes the houses were no more than low huts, but they usually had two or three rooms and a small yard. Stairs led to a flat roof where the family slept in hot weather. During the day, the roof could be used to dry fruit, such as figs and dates, in the sun.

Children worked alongside their parents, but also went to school, had toys, and played games. Boys played piggyback games, tug-of-war, and leapfrog. Girls danced, played with dolls, and adorned themselves with jewelry and makeup. When Egyptians kissed, they rubbed noses instead of touching lips.

People died younger than they do today and married younger, too. Couples married when the girls were about 12 and the boys about 15. Although husband and wife called each other "brother" and "sister," marriage between siblings did not occur in ordinary families as it did in the royal family.

The Egyptian women of the Old Kingdom work at home. While their children play, they perform the household jobs, which include making beer and mashing vegetables. Their main task, however, is to make fresh bread each day. They grind grain to make flour, add water, and mix in some of yesterday's uncooked bread to make the dough rise. Then they form it into different-shaped loaves, which are slapped onto the walls of their clay ovens or dropped into the hot ashes.

The flour is full of dirt and dung, so people often suffer from stomach pains. The grit in the bread wears down their teeth, so they also have toothaches.

Makeup

Among the upper classes, the highlight of the day was the evening feast. Egyptians, especially the men, took great care in dressing. Often they began to prepare themselves in the afternoon. They rubbed oil and perfumes onto their skin and shaved their bodies with bronze razors. On some days, for health reasons, they purged themselves, taking a laxative of senna and fruit to empty their bowels.

Many Egyptians wore wigs as a symbol of their importance, but they also took care

of their own hair, rubbing it with such substances as gazelle dung and hippopotamus fat to make it grow and the blood of a black bull to prevent it from turning white.

It was important to smell nice, because body odor was a sign of sinfulness. Women chewed honey pills to make their breath sweet. Men and women sprinkled their clothes with a perfume made from myrrh, frankincense, and fragrant plants. Finally, a servant, called the chief anointer, placed a cone on top of each person's head. It was soaked with sweet-smelling ointment that slowly melted over their wig during the warm night. This way, they were sure to smell as nice at the end of the evening as they did at the beginning.

Fashionable Egyptians wear eye makeup, wigs, jewelry, and incense cones. Around their eyes they use kohl, a black eyeliner made from crushed lead ore (inset, left), and blue or green eye shadow. Green is made from powdered copper ore.

The ladies of Chephren's court wear red lip salve and also paint their toenails and fingernails red. Necklaces, bracelets, and anklets complete their outfits.

Makeup, made from precious ointments and colorings, is mixed on a palette with a duck-shaped handle and applied with a stick (inset, left).

The Feast

In the Old Kingdom, court officials and their families lived with the pharaoh in the palace of the White Wall. Some richer officials also owned summer houses, where they could go to relax.

Official feasts were held to celebrate all the main holy days, but often a wealthy man would order his servants to prepare a huge meal simply to entertain his friends. At such a feast his *ka* (spirit of generosity) would make him "stretch out his arms in hospitality." Servants offered the guests beef, goat, antelope, goose, and duck, all cooked with imported herbs and spices. The meal was accompanied by wine and four kinds of beer.

Guests ate with their fingers. They also crushed lotus flowers between their fingers to savor the scent. Smell was important to the Egyptians; the drawing of a nose in Egyptian writing meant "smell," "taste," and also "enjoy." At a feast perfumes, flowers, food, and spices scented the air.

Toward the end of the evening, singers, acrobats, and magicians would entertain the guests. Young women performed slow, elegant dances. Nobody knows exactly what ancient Egyptian music sounded like, but pictures show musicians playing harps, lutes, zithers, and the sistrum (a metal rattle).

Special texts, written on papyrus, told Egyptians how to behave at feasts. They advised guests to look at their food, so that no one would think they were being stared at. A polite guest, they taught, spoke only when spoken to and laughed when others laughed. "This is how it is in Egypt," explained one manual of good behavior, "and only a fool would complain about it."

At a noble's feast, men and women sit apart. The guests will stay seated all night and will not join in the dancing or singing. They believe that mealtimes are precious to the gods and require good manners.

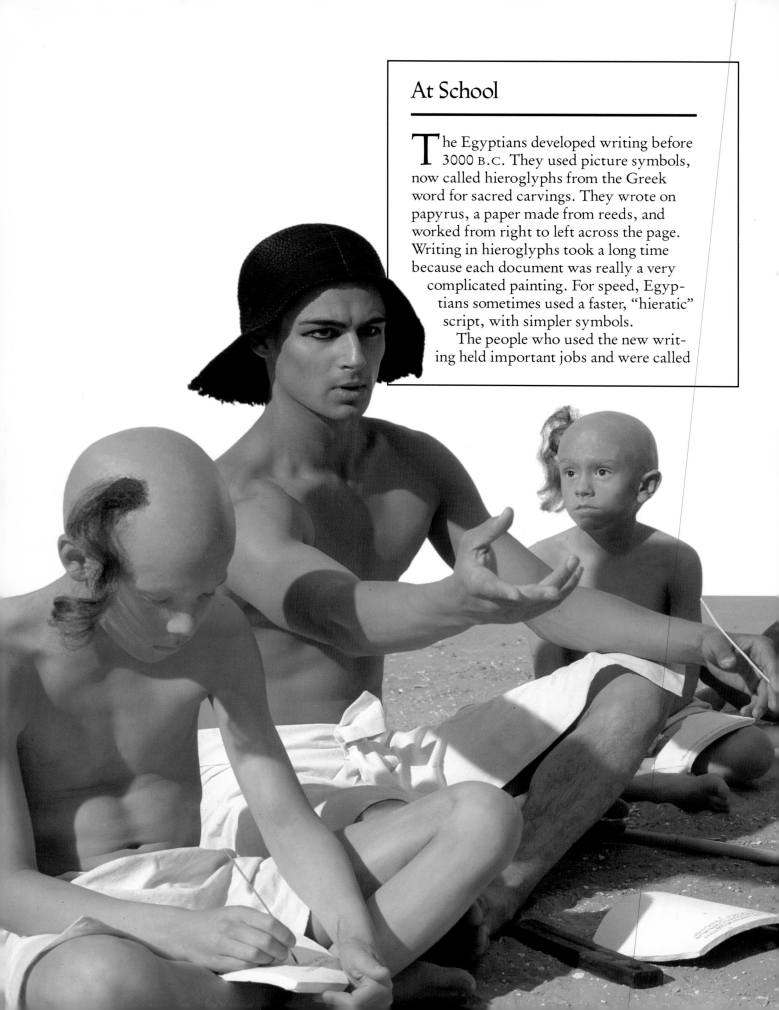

At School

The Egyptians developed writing before 3000 B.C. They used picture symbols, now called hieroglyphs from the Greek word for sacred carvings. They wrote on papyrus, a paper made from reeds, and worked from right to left across the page. Writing in hieroglyphs took a long time because each document was really a very complicated painting. For speed, Egyptians sometimes used a faster, "hieratic" script, with simpler symbols.

The people who used the new writing held important jobs and were called scribes. The hieroglyph for "scribe" was a drawing of a paint palette with red and black paint, a water pot, and a brush.

All Egyptian children went to school when they were four years old. At 12 most left school. The boys began to learn their fathers' trades, while the girls helped their mothers in the house. The sons of officials who were to become scribes went on studying for several years. Some girls also stayed on and became scribes, but in the Old Kingdom people often mocked the writings of women.

Many careers were open to the scribes. They might work for the Army or the Treasury. They could go into medicine, the priesthood, or architecture. Teachers encouraged their students to work hard. The life of a scribe is better than most, one old document says. The scribe is his own boss, whereas "the metalsmith works in the heat of the furnace. He stinks like rotten fish eggs."

The scholars learn proverbs and stories by heart and copy texts onto specially prepared pieces of pottery and limestone slates.

They learn reading, writing, and arithmetic, and older pupils study geography and history. Teachers emphasize memorization. Questioning and lack of respect are punished, sometimes by beating.

Sometimes the pupils whisper and daydream and long for noon, when their mothers will bring them a meal of bread and barley wine.

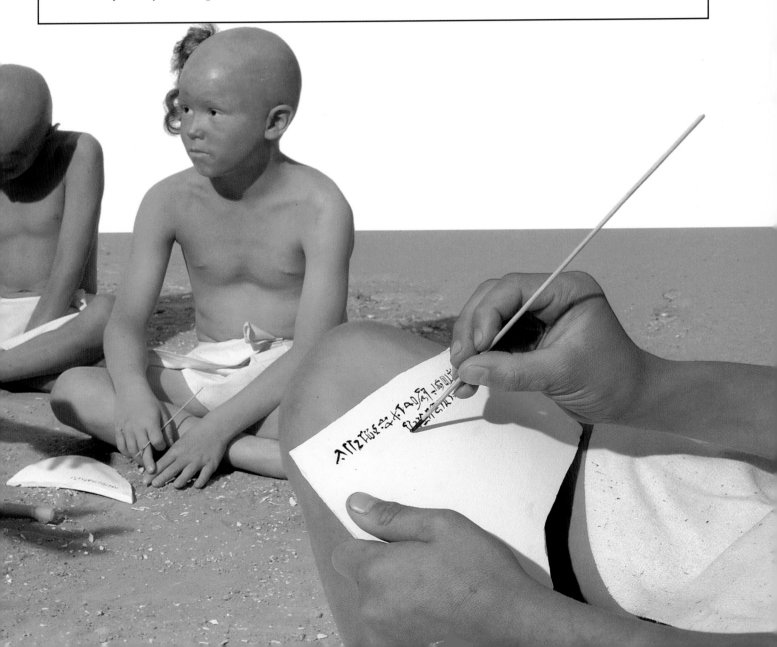

At the Doctor's

In the Old Kingdom, medicine was a combination of magic and science.

Doctors had papyrus texts describing how to examine the patient and diagnose disease; they looked for symptoms such as "blood like fried pig's blood." They were experts at bandaging and first aid. Some of their medicines contained healing substances that are still used today.

Often, however, doctors were powerless to relieve pain or prevent death. In such cases they tried magical cures. For example, the ointment for blindness contained a pig's eye because the doctors believed it had the strength of sight. They also prescribed spells and charms of stinking herbs and fish as protection against the spirits.

Patients might ask a doctor to advise them on how to get rid of fleas or even how to make clothes smell sweet. Doctors were thought to be wise and to know all the answers.

"You are going blind," the doctor tells this noble, "but this is a disease I can treat." He takes a pig's eye, some red ochre, and honey and grinds them together. He pours the ointment into the patient's ear then recites a spell twice: "I have applied this ointment to the trouble spot; you will see again."

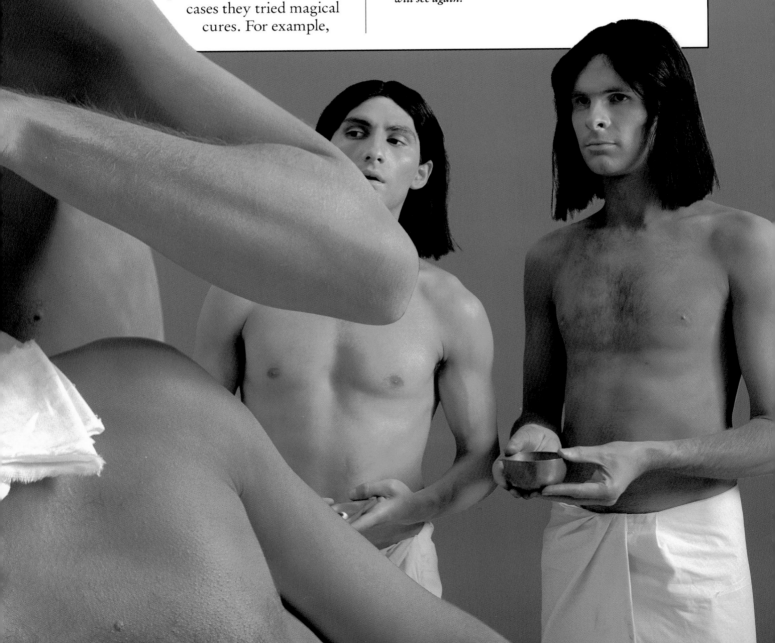

Hunting

B oth rich and poor hunted in ancient Egypt. The poor trapped birds and fish with different kinds of nets. Nobles hunted marsh birds with throw sticks (somewhat like boomerangs) and fished with harpoons. Using these ancient weapons required great skill. The rich also ventured courageously out in small papyrus boats to hunt fierce, strong hippopotami with harpoons and ropes.

Nobles also went hunting in the desert. They chased leopards, lions, and gazelles with hunting dogs and hoped to kill one of the mythical beasts of the desert: the sphinx, with the head of a man and the body of a lion; or a *sag*, half lion, half hawk. The minister in charge of the desert nome held the title Master of the Hunt.

Some animals were killed for food, some were killed for sacrifice to the gods, but others were kept alive. Lions were sacrificed to the Nile god so he would make the flood rise again, but when the nobles lassoed ibex and antelope, they reared them as domestic animals. Captured monkeys became ladies' pets, and baboons were used as guard animals in the markets.

Hunting was more than sport. In the legend of Horus, Seth the evil god had hidden in the body of a hippopotamus. Seth was also thought to live in the animals of the desert. By killing these animals, the Egyptians reenacted the victory of Horus over Seth, or the triumph of civilization over disorder.

As the hunters return home through the village with a catch of wildfowl, a young nobleman aims a throwstick at a bird. In the background, two peasants carry a sack of grain they'll use to pay their taxes.

Pharaoh's Decision

———————————————

Chephren ruled Egypt as Re ruled the gods. His power was divinely sanctioned and unquestioned. A chief minister who was permitted to nose (kiss) the pharaoh's feet had been granted the highest honor. Touching the pharaoh's crown or scepter, even accidentally, carried the death penalty.

The pharaoh controlled all trade. Each day he examined the accounts and reports, dictated letters to his scribes, and issued commands. He sent traders to Cush (Ethiopia), Punt (Somalia), and Byblos (Lebanon); miners to Sinai; and armies to Nubia (Sudan) and Libya.

Chephren's life was shaped by religious rituals. He woke at dawn and was washed by the women of his harem (the court of his wives). Each day he attended long religious services and offered food to his ancestors. Before his own meals, he washed again, rinsed his mouth, and changed clothes. He even ate according to ritual and ceremony because his meal was considered an offering to a god. The pharaoh's chief duty was to build and maintain temples to the gods.

Sometimes when Chephren gave commands he did not speak himself, but let officials speak for him. These court officials were called the Mouth, the Tongue, and the Repeater. Perhaps in such a way, one day in about 2555 B.C., Pharaoh Chephren announced his decision to build a pyramid.

Mahnud Hotep, imakhu, *architect, and High Priest of the god Ptah (the god of craftsmen), is summoned before Chephren. He is formally appointed Great Chief of Works in charge of building the pyramid that will be called "Great is Chephren."*

Finding True North

Mahnud Hotep's first task as the Great Chief of Works was to draw up the plans for Chephren's pyramid. An ancient story taught that when the pharaoh died his soul would become a bird that would fly off with a lamp in its beak and become a star in the northern sky. To help the soul find its way, the pyramid had to be aligned with the Pole Star so that it would face north.

Because the heavens were the home of the gods, Egyptian priests studied the stars carefully. They used astrology to calculate the lucky and unlucky days of the month and to determine when the gods' festivals should occur. These priests had an accurate calendar by 4000 B.C., a thousand years before the birth of Abraham. (The official Egyptian calendar was less successful. Lacking leap years, it was correct only once every 1,460 years!)

When the priests had worked out the correct alignment of the pyramid, Chephren and Mahnud Hotep visited Giza on a lucky day. Following the ceremonies laid down in *The Book of Temple Building* (which they believed was written by Imhotep, the architect of the first pyramid), they marked out the four corners of the site and put tools and charms underneath a foundation stone.

The priest, who is called "the watcher of time," carries a bay (palm stick). He takes a sighting on the Pole Star, lining up the star and the bay held by his servant. The line between them is true north. His measurements are so precise that the least accurate side of the pyramid is off by only one twelfth of one degree.

Leveling the Base

After the ceremony of measuring and staking the site, a team of workers cleared the sand and began to level the rock beneath it. The base of Chephren's pyramid covered 11 acres, and it was built on a slope. Knowing that water finds its own level, the workers dug a system of trenches and filled them with water. By marking the waterline,

they obtained a horizontal measurement that permitted them to level the entire area.

Meanwhile other workers cut a short, sloping tunnel underneath the site. When they were 16 feet (5 meters) underground, they cut a small chamber into its east wall. A large granite stone was wedged into the tunnel ceiling so that later it could be dropped down to seal the passage.

The masons then dug a second, larger chamber in the center of the base. This became Chephren's burial chamber. Its walls were smoothed with polishing stones and chisels. From this chamber, the workers dug a tunnel out toward the edge of the pyramid's base.

Nobody knows why the workers built two underground chambers. Perhaps their plans changed during construction, or the first tunnel was meant to confuse grave robbers.

Workers level the rock to make a flat base for the pyramid. They have no machines or power tools, only hand tools made either of copper or a hard rock called dolerite. Because the copper tools are quickly worn down, a team of metalworkers is kept busy sharpening old tools and making new ones.

34

At the Quarry

Most of the stone blocks for the pyramid came from limestone quarries near Giza. Up to 1,000 men, divided into gangs, worked in the quarries. Each gang had a name. One of the stones in the Great Pyramid still has the tally mark of one of the gangs: "Craftsmen Gang. How strong is the Crown of Cheops!"

In the quarries, the men cut the sides of a block, using copper chisels. Then they chipped holes at the base and hammered in wedges of dry wood. When it was moistened, the wood expanded. This forced the block upward, cracking the limestone across its bottom.

The gangs squared the blocks crudely with dolerite pounders. Large blocks were cut in half with a copper saw. When sawing, workers poured wet sand into the groove to act as an abrasive and make the cutting easier.

Other gangs brought the casing stones for the outside of the pyramid from the quarries at Tura, on the opposite bank of the Nile. In the Tura quarries, the highest quality stone lay deep in the hillside, so the men had to work in underground tunnels. Cut blocks were stored until the time of *akhet,* when workers put them on barges and rowed across the flooded river to the Giza pyramids.

Egyptians used granite, which is stronger and harder than limestone, for pillars and roofing blocks in the pyramids. Workers quarried the heavy granite blocks (some weighed 50 tons) 500 miles (800 kilometers) upriver from Giza, at Aswan. There the neighboring Nubians frequently attacked the Egyptian workers, so Chephren had to send soldiers to protect them. No one went to Aswan by choice; they had to be conscripted (ordered).

Gangs of workmen haul blocks of stone toward the River Nile. Each block weighs nearly three tons.

The First Layer

Most of the workers lived beside the pyramid in the barracks, a huge building made of rough limestone, with mud floors. They worked six hours a day, resting at midday when it was too hot to work, and returned to the barracks at night. The barracks had 91 rooms, each measuring 88 × 10 feet (27 × 3 meters). Up to 4,000 men could sleep there.

To the south of the pyramid was a small village. Here, with their families, lived the hundreds of craftsmen — the stonemasons, sculptors, artists, and surveyors — who worked on the pyramid. The village had no wells; water was carried from the river and poured into a cistern. In later times the cistern had to be guarded to stop people from stealing the water.

Sanitation was a problem at the site. The smell of sewage, refuse, and the nearby mortuary was appalling. When the wind came from a certain direction, the stench would even waft upstream to the palace of the White Wall.

The foreman of the gang carries a stick. His gang drags the block up the ramp by sheer force, since the Egyptians do not have cranes or pulleys. Although the block weighs over two tons, the weight is divided among the men, and the sledge runners are oiled, which makes moving the block easier. For each man it is about the same as pulling a child along on a sled.

The men call themselves the Scorpion Gang. Off duty they carve graffiti onto the blocks, boasting that they are the hardest-working group.

Roofing the Burial Chamber

Laying the 30,000 blocks in the bottom layer of the pyramid took at least a month. The workers then prepared to position roofing slabs over the burial chamber.

Before they could do this, however, they had to lower the pharaoh's sarcophagus (stone coffin) into the chamber, because it was too large to be taken down the entrance tunnel. They filled the chamber with 1,000 tons of sand and dragged the sarcophagus onto the top. Then they scooped out the sand. As they lowered the sand level, the coffin descended into the chamber. Finally, workers maneuvered it into a hole that they had cut for it in the floor of the burial chamber.

When this was done, workers again filled the room with sand in order to position the roof slabs. Using wooden rollers, they dragged the slabs across the first layer of the pyramid, then levered them onto the sand. One unfortunate gang then had to carry the 1,000 tons of sand out of the chamber through the entrance passage.

When it is finished, the weight of the entire pyramid will press down onto the roof slabs of the burial chamber, so they must be positioned perfectly. They are placed in a shallow, upside-down **V**, *so that the weight of the pyramid presses outward onto the walls of the burial chamber.*

Halfway There

Two thousand years after the time of Chephren, a Greek writer named Herodotus claimed that Chephren and Cheops were tyrants who enslaved the Egyptians and forced them to work on the pyramids. He claimed that "100,000 men labored constantly, relieved every month by a fresh lot."

Scholars now think that, at most, only 8,000 people could have worked on the pyramid site at any one time. If more had been involved, they would have gotten in one other's way. Nor were the workers unwilling slaves. Although they were made to work hard and the overseers were strict, they believed that the pharaoh was a god who protected the land, and that his eternal safety was everybody's concern. Also, they were paid in food at a time when the flooded fields could not produce crops.

Chephren's pyramid was 708 feet (216 meters) square at its base and contained over two million blocks of stone. It is difficult to imagine the organization needed to build so large a structure.

Although thousands of workers were

conscripted to do the unskilled laboring jobs, most of them were only available during the four months of *akhet*. To build such a pyramid in 20 years, a thousand blocks a day had to be put in place — three every minute. As the pyramid grew, workers had to haul the blocks up long ramps before they could position them. Because of its shape, only 4 percent of the blocks remained to be dragged into position when the pyramid reached two-thirds of its final height. But that meant the laborers still had to pull up about 80,000 more blocks.

Adding to the amount of work to be done, Chephren had ordered the construction of a smaller pyramid south of his own. Now almost totally destroyed, it was 65 feet (20 meters) square and 42 feet (13 meters) high. Although it is sometimes called a "queen's pyramid," the entrance is so small that an adult can hardly get into it. It was probably built for religious reasons.

The overseer works late into the evening planning the next day's schedule. The pyramid is a marvel of Egyptian organization: over 100 gangs work together, but there is no confusion.

41

Accident!

A pyramid may look simple to build, but the immense weight of the stone can make it very unstable. Imhotep, who designed the first pyramid, discovered how to spread the weight and make the pyramid more stable by constructing dozens of buttresses (vertical columns of blocks) inside the pyramid, 8 feet (2.5 meters) apart.

Even so, not all pyramids were successfully completed. Chephren's grandfather, Seneferu, seems to have built three pyramids. The pyramid at Meidum had buttresses only every 16 feet (5 meters) and it collapsed, perhaps after a rainstorm. The roof of a chamber inside the Bent Pyramid cracked during building, forcing the builders to change the angle of the sides halfway up to reduce the pyramid's final height. The casing stones fell off the nearby Red Pyramid. These incidents make the successful construction of Chephren's pyramid all the more remarkable.

A moment's inattention and a pyramid becomes a dangerous place. Every day, site doctors treat a succession of cut fingers, crushed toes, and broken limbs. Only a lucky gang can boast that not one of its men has died during the building of the pyramid.

Royal Statues

Before sculptors began work on a statue for the pyramid site, various religious ceremonies had to be performed. Next, a draftsman drew a grid of squares on the surface of the stone. Then on each side of the block he drew an outline of the pharaoh, from the front, sides, and back. The knee was always drawn in the sixth square, the shoulders in the thirteenth. Such rules, laid down in *The Book of the Artist*, explain why Egyptian statues do not look realistic.

The sculptors chipped back the profiles from each side until they met in the middle. Apprentices did the unskilled work at the beginning, and the Director of Sculptors added the finishing touches. Reserve heads were also made and placed in the pyramid

in case Chephren's corpse was damaged.

Finally, sculptors inscribed the hieroglyphs of the names of Chephren on the base of the statue. When this was done, the Egyptians believed, the statue became Chephren. In later times wealthy Egyptians, rather than paying for their own statues, sometimes just chipped out the first name and added their own. They believed it then became a statue of them.

Sculptors in the royal workshops carve the diorite statues of the pharaoh that will be placed in the Valley Temple of the pyramid, on the banks of the Nile. Some of the statues are finished and await only the ceremony of the Opening of the Mouth to bring them to life.

The statues do not represent Chephren as he is — an old man about to die — but show the idealized face and body of a young man. The statues in the background have falcons carved on their shoulders, because the falcon represents the god Horus.

Casing and Finishing

Chephren's pyramid had 124 layers of stone. On top the builders placed a large granite capstone. With the capstone in place, the pyramid stood 471 feet (144 meters) high.

Working from the top of the pyramid to the bottom, workers then positioned hundreds of casing blocks. Most of the blocks were white limestone brought from the quarries at Tura, but some, used at the base of the pyramid, were red granite from Aswan. Nearby, sculptors carved a rocky outcrop into a giant sphinx, a lion with a human head. Although its head has since been damaged, the face appears to have Chephren's features.

Over the years most of the casing blocks have been stolen for building stone; many were used to build the great mosque in Cairo in the sixteenth century. Only a few near the top of the pyramid remain in place.

Masons smooth and square the edges of one of the limestone casing blocks. It must be correctly positioned within a fraction of an inch.

When the masons have finished, priests, using plumb lines, will check that the angle of the slope is precisely correct (52.3 degrees). Laborers will then rub the casing blocks with polishing stones until they shine in the sun, and sculptors will inscribe them with hundreds of hieroglyphs describing Chephren's entry into heaven to rule with the gods.

The Last Journey

The Egyptians believed that the dead went to the Kingdom of the West, a land ruled by the god Osiris. Many of the funeral ceremonies were derived from the story of Osiris.

According to the myth, Osiris was chopped into pieces by his brother Seth, who scattered his body all over Egypt. Isis, the wife of Osiris, searched for the body and gathered the pieces together. They were then mummified, and each part was buried in a different place. Using magic, Isis made each part turn into a whole body. Her son Horus touched the mouth of each body, so that it came to life. Horus then killed Seth. Although Horus was blinded in one eye during the battle, his sight was restored, and he was made pharaoh of Egypt.

The death of the pharaoh was traumatic for the Egyptians, because they believed the pharaoh was the god Horus, who protected Egypt. When the pharaoh died, they felt as alone as a child lost in the desert. Inside the palace men sat with their heads on their knees. Women let their dresses hang down off their shoulders. They wailed and sprinkled dirt on their heads. Professional mourners sang funeral songs.

The religious ceremonies were strictly observed. Without them the Egyptians believed Chephren could not be reborn, and the new pharaoh could not begin to reign.

Pharaoh Chephren has died. Priests perform the ceremony of "searching" for the body, in the same way that Isis searched for Osiris. Then the dead pharaoh is carried from the palace of the White Wall to the royal barge. The procession is led by the Lector Priest. He reads: "The stars weep and the dead tremble, because pharaoh has risen to the horizon."

The crown prince walks behind the priest. In the background, servants carry Chephren's possessions, which they believe he will need in the afterlife.

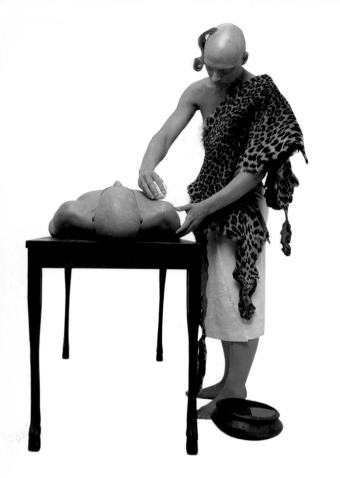

Mummification

Wealthy Egyptians were mummified after death, because they believed they would need their bodies in the afterlife.

Although poor people could not afford to be mummified, they were buried naked in the desert sand on their left sides, facing west. The sand dried out their bodies and preserved them just as effectively as the processes of mummification. Their families buried tools, jewelry, and bowls of food with them, showing that they hoped to go to the Kingdom of Osiris.

When Chephren died, his body was laid on a funeral boat, under a canopy. A lamp burned in the bow. At either end stood two female mourners, representing the goddesses Isis and Nephthys, the protector of

the dead. The body was taken down the Nile to Giza. The Egyptians believed that this short voyage represented the journey that the pharaoh would soon take across the marshes to heaven.

At Giza, the body was mummified. Mummification took about 70 days and was carried out by special priests who belonged to the Guild of Embalmers. The ceremonies were based on the myth of Osiris. The man who cut open the abdomen to remove the internal organs — the ripper — was stoned and driven away, perhaps because he reminded the onlookers of Seth, who chopped up the body of Osiris.

Priests washed the body, preserved it in natron (a type of salt), and bandaged it, just as Isis had preserved the body of Osiris. The stoppers of the four canopic jars (in which the liver, lungs, stomach, and intestines were placed) were carved into animal heads

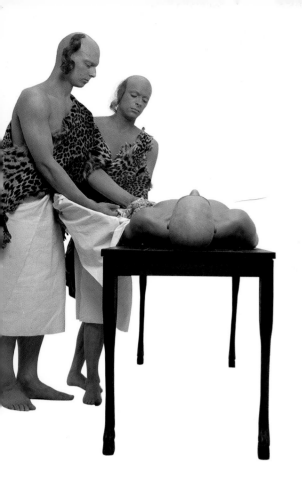

representing the four gods who the Egyptians believed protected the internal organs.

Priests wash the corpse in the ibu *(purifying place), symbolizing its rebirth from the dead (above, far left). Then they rub the body with natron to dry and preserve the skin (above left).*

The body is taken to the wabt *(mummifying tent), where priests protect the face by coating it with resin. They remove the internal organs, which will rot quickly (above). These are dried out with natron crystals, wrapped in cloth soaked in liquid natron, and put into four canopic jars to be buried near the pharaoh.*

Next, priests rub the corpse with perfumes and oils. They push bandages, resins, natron, and sawdust into the stomach to fill it out (above right).

After this, they bandage each part of the body individually, as Isis bandaged Osiris. Sometimes the linen bandages are cut to look like clothing or even a false beard. Sweet-smelling resins glue and stiffen them.

The priests take great care to avoid damaging the head. They try to make the face look as lifelike as possible, although the bandages covering it are painted green — the traditional color of Osiris's face (right).

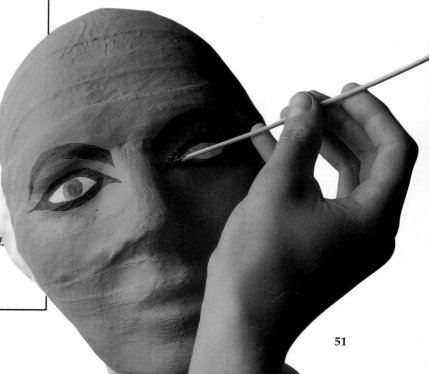

51

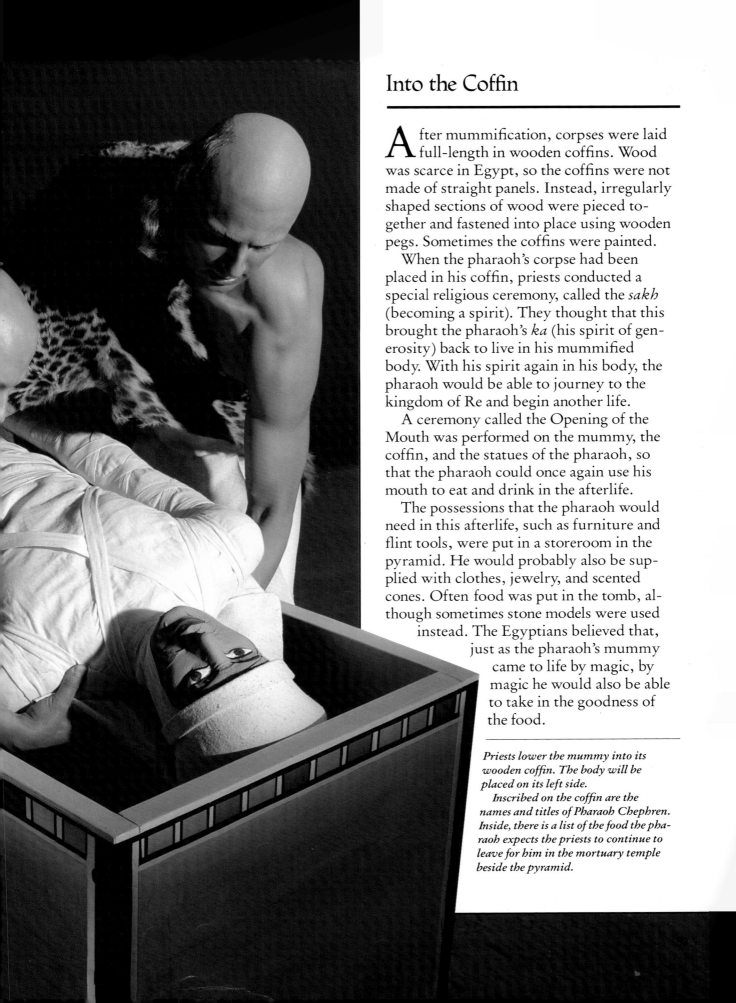

Into the Coffin

After mummification, corpses were laid full-length in wooden coffins. Wood was scarce in Egypt, so the coffins were not made of straight panels. Instead, irregularly shaped sections of wood were pieced together and fastened into place using wooden pegs. Sometimes the coffins were painted.

When the pharaoh's corpse had been placed in his coffin, priests conducted a special religious ceremony, called the *sakh* (becoming a spirit). They thought that this brought the pharaoh's *ka* (his spirit of generosity) back to live in his mummified body. With his spirit again in his body, the pharaoh would be able to journey to the kingdom of Re and begin another life.

A ceremony called the Opening of the Mouth was performed on the mummy, the coffin, and the statues of the pharaoh, so that the pharaoh could once again use his mouth to eat and drink in the afterlife.

The possessions that the pharaoh would need in this afterlife, such as furniture and flint tools, were put in a storeroom in the pyramid. He would probably also be supplied with clothes, jewelry, and scented cones. Often food was put in the tomb, although sometimes stone models were used instead. The Egyptians believed that, just as the pharaoh's mummy came to life by magic, by magic he would also be able to take in the goodness of the food.

Priests lower the mummy into its wooden coffin. The body will be placed on its left side.

Inscribed on the coffin are the names and titles of Pharaoh Chephren. Inside, there is a list of the food the pharaoh expects the priests to continue to leave for him in the mortuary temple beside the pyramid.

Opening of the Mouth

The doorways of the valley temple were inscribed with Chephren's name and titles. Sunlight reflected off the white alabaster floor. Twenty-three statues of Chephren stood in the temple. Before the pharaoh was entombed, the statues were "brought to life" by the Opening of the Mouth ceremony. The Egyptians believed that this gave the *ka* of the dead pharaoh 23 resting places in addition to the mummified body.

After this ceremony, Chephren's coffin was taken up a covered ramp to the mortuary temple beside the pyramid. The ramp was a quarter of a mile (400 meters) long, lit by slits in the roof. In the temple a bull was killed and prayers were said. The priests believed that the strength of the bull would help Chephren rise from the dead.

Finally, Chephren's coffin was carried along the tunnel to the burial chamber inside the pyramid and lowered into the stone sarcophagus. The lid of the sarcophagus was sealed in place. Only then could the crown prince take the throne and assume the title of pharaoh.

The Opening of the Mouth ceremony gives life to the many statues of Pharaoh Chephren, just as Horus and Isis gave life to the many pieces of Osiris's body.

The ceremony is performed by priests, including the crown prince (right), the son of the dead pharaoh.

The priests sprinkle the statue with water, wave incense over it, and offer sacrifice. They touch its mouth with a chisel and a tool called an adz. They then rub milk on its lips and dress it in royal clothes.

54

The Pharaoh at Rest

The Egyptians had several different ideas about what would happen to Chephren when his mummified body was placed in the pyramid.

According to the priests of Re, the pharaoh would go to heaven, to rule with Re in the kingdom of the gods. Ancient texts describe his arrival: "The bolts of the doors fly open. He eats the gods for his meals." In heaven he would become one of the *imakhu* of Re and would help Re take the sun across the sky.

According to the priests of Osiris, the pharaoh would go to rule the Kingdom of Osiris in the west. There he would become Osiris. As the pharaoh, Chephren had been the god Horus. After his death, however, his son would rule in Egypt. Chephren, as the father of the new pharaoh Horus, became Osiris.

As Osiris, Chephren would use his divine power to defend Egypt and the new pharaoh. This explains why Chephren's pyramid was so massive. It was a fortress designed to keep his mummified body safe, so that he could continue to protect Egypt.

The pyramid failed in its task. When an Italian, Giovanni Belzoni, rediscovered the entrance in 1818, he found the storeroom empty and the tomb open. The polished granite lid of the sarcophagus lay broken on the floor. Chephren's body had been removed.

The crown prince and the priests leave the burial chamber and seal the tunnel leading to it. They have even brushed their footsteps off the floor. Above, thousands of tons of masonry protect Chephren's body. In the royal chamber of Chephren's pyramid all is quiet.

Offerings to the Dead

To ensure Chephren's eternal safety, priests regularly performed religious ceremonies at the mortuary temple, even after his burial. Their most important task was to provide food for his *ka;* Chephren did not want to be like the neglected dead, who it was believed went hungry and were forced to eat their own dung. Before he died, he set up farms to support his priests and to provide the food offerings. The *ka* priests were forbidden to do any other work.

The most flourishing business in the Old Kingdom was the business of death. Most Egyptian men worked on a pyramid at some time. Some worked there all their lives. A pharaoh building a pyramid was the biggest customer of the country's building, quarrying, and shipping industries. He was also the greatest patron of painters and sculptors and the most important employer of astronomers, architects, and mathematicians.

The vast scale of all this activity strained the Egyptian economy. Every pharaoh and noble who built a tomb added to the problem. Ministering to the dead used up a great amount of wealth, land, and food and left less for the living.

To become pure, a priest washes three times, puts on clean, white linen clothes, and shaves his body. He brings offerings of food for Chephren, placing them before a false door carved in the stone wall of the mortuary temple. Chephren's ka, *he believes, will come out to eat the offering.*

The Boat Pits

E ven after Chephren had been buried, work at the pyramid site did not stop. It was the duty of Chephren's son, Mycerinus, to complete the buildings around his father's pyramid while he started to build his own. A pyramid complex was usually too large an undertaking to be completed during the reign of one pharaoh.

It is probable that neither the valley temple nor the mortuary temple were finished when Chephren died. Craftsmen had yet to decorate the covered way that led between them. According to Herodotus, who visited Giza in about 450 B.C., the walls were covered with painted reliefs. Perhaps they showed the glories of Chephren's reign, or scenes from everyday life.

Beside the mortuary temple, laborers dug six large boat pits. Modern archaeologists have found similar pits near a number of Egyptian graves. One was discovered in 1954 near the Great Pyramid of Cheops. When they opened the pit, the archaeologists could smell incense, 4,500 years old. In the pit was the pharaoh's royal boat. It had been dismantled into 1,224 pieces, but it was preserved well enough to be rebuilt.

Shipwrights dismantle the funeral boat which carried Chephren's body to Giza. The boat is made of cedar wood from Byblos (Lebanon). The planks are tied together with rope. Each is marked with a sign to show where it belonged—port, starboard, fore, or aft. The oars are left in place, and the ship faces west, ready to carry the pharaoh to the Kingdom of Osiris.

The pieces of the boat are laid in one of the six boat pits. This pit has been given a coating of plaster to make it airtight. Soon, stonemasons will drag large stone blocks into position to seal it.

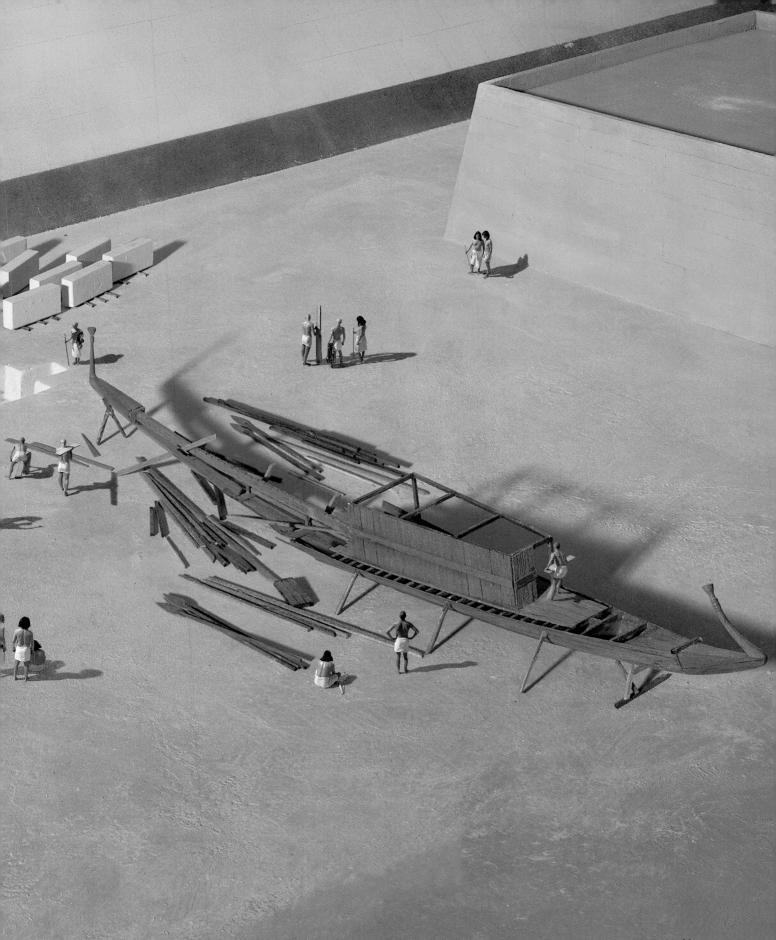

How Do We Know?

THE END OF THE ANCIENT EGYPTIANS

The ancient Egyptian civilization lasted for 2,000 years after the end of the Old Kingdom. Then, in 332 B.C., Egypt was conquered by the Greeks. Slowly, the ancient Egyptian culture and writing began to disappear. After A.D. 391 when the Romans took over from the Greeks and closed most of the Egyptian temples, people lost the ability to read hieroglyphs altogether.

JEWISH, GREEK, AND ROMAN SOURCES

For a long time the writings of the Israelites, Greeks, and Romans provided our only knowledge about the ancient Egyptians.

Descriptions of Egyptian life in the Old Testament stories of Joseph and Moses are similar to stories that Egyptians told, but they are biased against the Egyptians, particularly their religious practices. Despite this, Solomon's Proverbs resemble Egyptian maxims.

The Greeks, and later the Romans, made fun of the Egyptians, who worshiped eels instead of eating them and went to war because of a quarrel over a holy crocodile.

Their books, however, tell us a lot about the Egyptians. Manetho, an Egyptian who lived in Roman times, wrote a list of the pharaohs in 31 dynasties, which is still used today. Herodotus wrote an important account of Egypt in about 450 B.C., although historians recognize that he was writing 2,000 years after Chephren and that he spiced his books with tidbits of scandal.

HIEROGLYPHS AND ARCHAEOLOGY

For reliable information about the ancient Egyptians, we must turn to the writings and monuments of the Egyptians themselves.

In 1799 one of Napoleon's soldiers found the Rosetta Stone. It had the same inscription written three times: in Greek, in hieroglyphs, and in demotic (another form of Egyptian writing). The name Ptolmis occurred a number of times in the text, and scholars realized that the hieroglyphs that made up the name were always outlined by an oval cartouche. In 1822, by comparing the letters with those in the cartouche of Queen Kliopadrat (Cleopatra), Jean-François Champollion unlocked the meaning of the hieroglyphs. He was the first per-

son to understand them since A.D. 400.

Soon scholars realized that the Coptic language (which was still spoken in some Egyptian monasteries) was similar to the language spoken by the ancient Egyptians, 5,000 years before. Today, historians can read texts written by scribes who lived during Chephren's reign. They can read, for example, how an *imakhu* became the *tjaty*; what was brought back from an expedition to Nubia (Sudan); and what medicines were prescribed by Egyptian doctors. Hundreds of spells carved on the walls of certain pyramids — the pyramid texts — show what

Egyptians believed would happen to the pharaoh in the afterlife.

Meanwhile, archaeologists had begun to study the tombs, temples, and other remains of the ancient Egyptians.

CONTROVERSIES AND INTERPRETATION

For many years, little was known about the pyramids. People believed that they were observatories or granaries built by Joseph for the pharaoh or that they were used to measure the earth. With new information, we have a clearer understanding of their purpose. Yet some mysteries remain. Although we now know more about mummification, we still don't know where it took place during the Old Kingdom. Similarly, while we know why the pyramids were built, we don't know precisely how stones were gotten to the top. This book depicts a spiral of ramps around the pyramid. Another theory is that builders used one huge ramp. However, that ramp would have been over a mile long and a bigger building job than the pyramid itself!

We also don't know precisely what the men working on the pyramids looked like. Wall paintings and sculptures from the Old Kingdom offer some clues, suggesting that the Egyptian workers looked similar to peoples from neighboring countries to the north. But Egyptian art followed strict rules; it tended to make everyone look the same, so wall paintings and statues don't tell us much about differences in features or skin color. Historians disagree about whether the peoples of Egypt were generally descended from black Africans who lived to the south, or from the Semitic peoples of the Middle East. At the time this book takes place, during the Old Kingdom, many different groups were moving into the Nile valley, including Nubians from the South, Libyans, and even occasional Pygmies from central Africa. But many historians believe that the population of northern Egypt — those most likely to have worked in the crews at Giza — was still predominantly light-skinned during the Old Kingdom.

Ancient texts and archaeological remains offer facts and clues about the past, but historians are aware that these must be interpreted carefully to learn who the Egyptians were and what their lives were like. Perhaps one day, if you keep learning about ancient Egypt, you, too, may help unravel more of its secrets.

Index

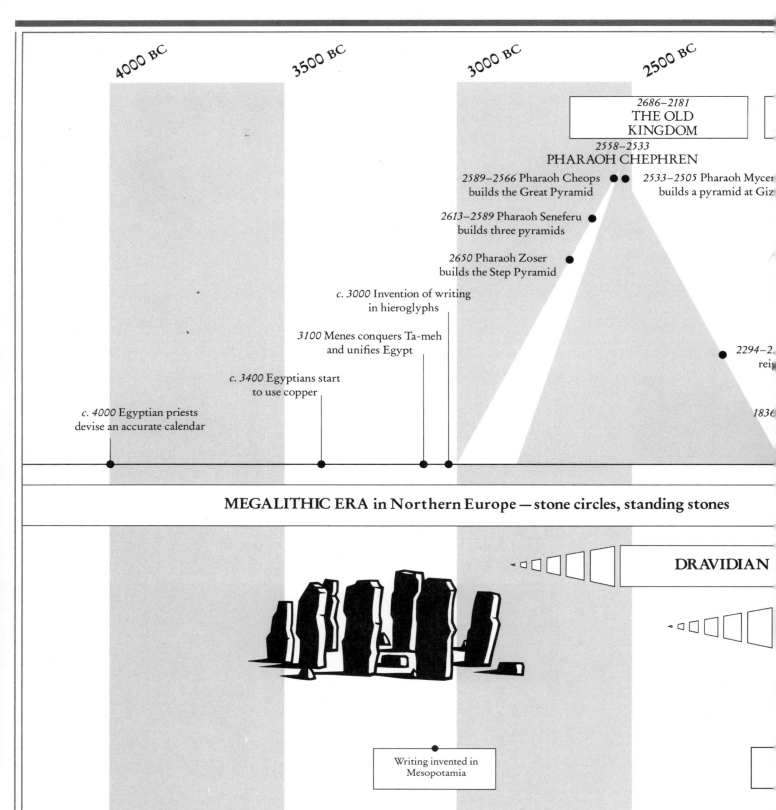

2686–2181
THE OLD
KINGDOM

2558–2533
PHARAOH CHEPHREN

2589–2566 Pharaoh Cheops
builds the Great Pyramid

2533–2505 Pharaoh Mycer
builds a pyramid at Giz

2613–2589 Pharaoh Seneferu
builds three pyramids

2650 Pharaoh Zoser
builds the Step Pyramid

c. 3000 Invention of writing
in hieroglyphs

3100 Menes conquers Ta-meh
and unifies Egypt

c. 3400 Egyptians start
to use copper

c. 4000 Egyptian priests
devise an accurate calendar

*2294–2.
reig

1836

MEGALITHIC ERA in Northern Europe — stone circles, standing stones

DRAVIDIAN

Writing invented in
Mesopotamia